W9-ASY-630

DISCARD

HOUSTON
TEXANS

by J Chris Roselius

Published by ABDO Publishing Company, 8000 West 78th Street, Edina, Minnesota 55439. Copyright © 2011 by Abdo Consulting Group, Inc. International copyrights reserved in all countries. No part of this book may be reproduced in any form without written permission from the publisher. SportsZone™ is a trademark and logo of ABDO Publishing Company.

Printed in the United States of America,
North Mankato, Minnesota
062010
092010

 THIS BOOK CONTAINS AT LEAST 10% RECYCLED MATERIALS.

Editor: Matt Tustison
Copy Editor: Nicholas Cafarelli
Interior Design and Production: Craig Hinton
Cover Design: Craig Hinton

Photo Credits: Evan Pinkus/AP Images, cover; NFL Photos/AP Images, title page, 15, 16, 19, 20, 24, 42 (top), 42 (middle), 42 (bottom), 44; Beth A. Keiser/AP Images, 4; David Stluka/AP Images, 7; Ed Reinke/AP Images, 8; John Bazemore/AP Images, 11, 36; AP Images, 12, 23; John Dickerson/AP Images, 27, 47; Spencer Weiner/AP Images, 28, 43 (top); Steven Senne/AP Images, 31; David Stluka/AP Images, 32; Alan Mothner/AP Images, 35; Darren Hauck/AP Images, 39, 43 (middle); John Amis/AP Images, 40, 43 (bottom)

Library of Congress Cataloging-in-Publication Data
Roselius, J Chris.
 Houston Texans / J. Chris Roselius.
   p. cm. — (Inside the NFL)
 Includes index.
 ISBN 978-1-61714-013-6
 1. Houston Texans (Football team)—History—Juvenile literature. I. Title.
 GV958.H69R67 2011
 796.332'64097641411—dc22
                              2010014965

TABLE OF CONTENTS

CHAPTER 1

WINNERS AT LAST

Since they had begun playing in the National Football League (NFL) as an expansion team in 2002, the Houston Texans had never been able to call themselves winners.

The best record the franchise had ever experienced was 8–8 in the 2007 and 2008 seasons. But as the Texans entered their final game in 2009, they were one victory away from finishing 9–7.

Just as important was the fact that a win would keep the Texans in the hunt for their first playoff appearance. Standing in their way, however, were the New England Patriots, one of the top teams in the NFL.

"I'm excited for our players," Houston coach Gary Kubiak said before the game. "That's what you work for—to be sitting here,

TIGHT END JOEL DREESSEN CELEBRATES DURING A 34–27 VICTORY IN THE 2009 FINALE. THE TEXANS WENT 9–7 FOR THEIR FIRST WINNING RECORD.

LEADER OF THE PACK

Houston quarterback Matt Schaub finished the 2009 season with 4,770 passing yards to lead the NFL. He showed why the Texans acquired him from the Atlanta Falcons before the 2007 season. Schaub was named to the American Football Conference (AFC) Pro Bowl team for his performance in 2009. He was then selected as the Most Valuable Player (MVP) for the game. It was played in Miami one week before the Super Bowl. Schaub threw for 189 yards and two touchdowns, including one to his Texans teammate Andre Johnson. The AFC team beat the National Football Conference (NFC) team 41–34.

the last game of the season, knowing when we walk out there Sunday, it means everything to our team.

"The thing that's hard—but I think it's good—is we're going to have to beat the top franchise in football to get to that point."

The host Texans started well. The more than 70,000 fans in attendance at Reliant Stadium were filled with hope.

Tight end Joel Dreessen hauled in a 25-yard pass from quarterback Matt Schaub to put Houston ahead 7–0.

New England came back to take a 10–7 lead by the second quarter. Texans safety Bernard Pollard then pounced on a fumble in the Patriots' end zone to give Houston a 13–10 lead.

Things took a turn for the worse for the Texans, however. The Patriots tied the score with a field goal right before halftime and then built a 27–13 lead in the fourth quarter.

All the fans who were cheering in the first half were now sitting in silence. There was no way their Texans were going to be able to come back and beat the Patriots, was there?

But just when it seemed that Houston's hopes of a

THE TEXANS' JACOBY JONES MAKES AN 8-YARD TOUCHDOWN CATCH AS PART OF A LATE RALLY IN THE LAST REGULAR-SEASON GAME OF THE 2009 SEASON.

winning season and possible playoff berth were dashed, the Texans started to rally.

Schaub moved the ball down the field, capping a drive with an 8-yard pass to Jacoby Jones for a touchdown. There was 9:41 left. Star defensive end Mario Williams sacked Patriots quarterback Tom Brady on third down to force a punt. Then Arian Foster scored on a 1-yard run for Houston. Kris Brown kicked the extra point to tie the score at 27.

SAFETY BERNARD POLLARD REACTS AFTER SCORING IN HIS TEAM'S 34–27 WIN TO END THE 2009 SEASON. HOUSTON JUST MISSED MAKING THE PLAYOFFS.

GETTING BETTER

Under coach Gary Kubiak, the Texans made steady improvement. In his first year as coach, in 2006, Houston went 6–10. This was four wins better than the team's 2005 record. In 2007, the Texans reached 8–8 for the first time. They then went 8–8 once again in 2008 before they finally broke .500 by going 9–7 in 2009.

With the game tied, the Texans needed the defense to come up with another big stand. The defense did exactly what it had to do. Pollard intercepted a pass after Brady was hit by Williams. Now Houston needed to score.

Riding a wave of momentum, the Texans marched toward the Patriots' end zone. With just less than two minutes remaining, Foster scampered into the end zone from 3 yards out to give Houston a lead. Brown's extra point put the Texans ahead 34–27. They held on to win by that score after the defense made one last stand.

When the game ended, the fans cheered wildly and the players hugged each other. The team had accomplished a first. The Texans had finished the season with a winning record.

"We're winners," cornerback Dunta Robinson said in a locker room full of enthusiastic players. "We're not right at .500. We're over .500. It's a great thing. I can say that I was a part of the first winning season for the Houston Texans. We're a part of something special."

All-Pro receiver Andre Johnson had six receptions for 65 yards. He had been a member of the Texans since 2003. The win was especially meaningful for him, after he had gone through so many tough seasons in Houston.

"I just started yelling," Johnson said about how he felt when the game was over. "It was like a sigh of relief. This is

BACK TO BACK

Texans wide receiver Andre Johnson finished the 2009 season with an NFL-leading 1,569 yards and was third in catches with 101. Johnson joined 2010 Hall of Fame inductee Jerry Rice as the only players since the merger of the American Football League (AFL) and NFL in 1970 to lead the league in receiving yards in back-to-back seasons. Rice did so in 1989 and 1990 and from 1993 to 1995. Johnson also became only the second receiver in NFL history to top 1,500 yards in back-to-back seasons. He joined former Indianapolis Colts wide receiver Marvin Harrison, who did so in 2001 and 2002.

SO CLOSE

To make the playoffs in 2009, the Texans needed a win in the last regular-season game and losses by Denver and either Baltimore or the New York Jets.

Houston did what it was supposed to do, beating New England in the regular-season finale, and Denver lost to Kansas City. Baltimore, however, defeated Oakland, and the Jets, playing on Sunday night, routed Cincinnati 37–0. The Bengals had already clinched a playoff spot. They did not have the same motivation that the Jets did. New York needed to win to make the postseason. Those results kept the Texans from making the playoffs.

"I'm disappointed with the way Cincinnati played," Texans owner Bob McNair said. "I thought that probably that game, the odds were a little more in our favor than any of the other games [Sunday]. As it turned out, they just left their game at home."

something that I've been working for since I've been here."

A few hours later, the New York Jets defeated the Cincinnati Bengals. As a result, the Texans fell short of the postseason. But they were still winners. Their brief past had featured disappointment. But the future appeared to be full of promise.

HOUSTON'S ANDRE JOHNSON MAKES A CATCH IN SEPTEMBER 2009. THE STAR WIDE RECEIVER SAID "IT WAS LIKE A SIGH OF RELIEF" TO FINALLY BE ON A WINNING TEAM.

CHAPTER 2

FOOTBALL RETURNS TO HOUSTON

On October 6, 1999, the city of Houston rejoiced. After suffering through the departure of the Houston Oilers for Tennessee in 1996, football was coming back. The league had approved Houston businessman Bob McNair's $700 million bid for an expansion team.

The new team would begin play in 2002. McNair and the city of Houston beat out Los Angeles to receive the league's 32nd franchise.

"It's an awful lot of money," McNair said after the vote by the league's owners. "But we've got a tremendous product in NFL football, and a stadium that'll knock your socks off."

"This is a great day for Houston," said mayor Lee Brown, who announced the news to applause

TEXANS OWNER BOB MCNAIR SHOWS OFF THE NEW TEAM'S LOGO IN 2000. MCNAIR BOUGHT THE EXPANSION TEAM FOR $700 MILLION IN 1999.

TEXANS, PART 5

When Houston owner Bob McNair unveiled the team nickname of Texans, it was not the first time a professional football team had that name. In 1952, there was an NFL team called the Dallas Texans that played for one year. From 1960 to 1962, Dallas again was the home of a team called the Texans. That team played in the AFL before moving to Kansas City and becoming the Chiefs. In 1974, Houston was home to a team called the Texans that played in the World Football League. Finally, the San Antonio Texans played in the Canadian Football League in 1995.

and cheers at the city council's regular meeting. "Today, we scored a touchdown for our fans, for our community, and for our economy."

The road to landing a new team was not a smooth one for McNair. He had started his quest to get an NFL team back in Houston only months after the Oilers, who are now the Tennessee Titans, left. Hindering McNair and the city was

the fact that the NFL was very public about wanting a team in Los Angeles. Los Angeles is the second-largest city in the United States. Houston had a stadium plan in place and an owner who was committed to keeping the team in the city. But the NFL was giving Los Angeles every chance possible to land the new club.

In March 1999, the NFL Expansion Committee voted 29–2 to give Los Angeles six months to work on a stadium plan and find an ownership group. In the end, the league was not satisfied with any of the possible Los Angeles team owners or stadium plans. Houston was awarded the 32nd NFL team.

"On balance," said Paul Tagliabue, the NFL commissioner at the time, "Houston was superior."

RELIANT STADIUM WAS THE NFL'S FIRST STADIUM WITH A RETRACTABLE ROOF. BUILDING BEGAN IN EARLY 2000, AND THE FACILITY OPENED IN 2002.

For three years, football fans had been waiting for the return of the NFL. Thanks to McNair, those fans got their wish. But being awarded a team was just the start of a three-year process to turn the idea of a team into an actual one. The first step was

DID YOU KNOW?

After unveiling the team's name, logo, and colors on September 6, 2000, Texans owner Bob McNair threw the first pitch that night before the Houston Astros of Major League Baseball played host to the Florida Marlins. However, instead of throwing a baseball to Astros owner Drayton McLane, McNair threw a football.

DOM CAPERS, SHOWN IN 2003, WAS HIRED AS THE TEXANS' FIRST COACH IN 2001. HE HAD EXPERIENCE COACHING AN EXPANSION TEAM WITH THE CAROLINA PANTHERS.

taken on January 19, 2000. That is when Charley Casserly was hired as the executive vice president/general manager. While Casserly was placed in charge of hiring front office executives and a head coach, the team still had no name.

By February of 2000, thousands of ideas for possible team names had been narrowed to five: Apollos, Bobcats, Stallions, Texans, and Wildcatters. Bobcats and Wildcatters were the first names to be dropped from the list of finalists. This happened as the groundbreaking for the NFL's first retractable-roof stadium got underway. The new stadium is located right next to the famed Astrodome, where the Oilers played. With the help of fans' voting online, the official team name of Texans was unveiled in front of thousands of fans at a downtown rally on September 6, 2000.

Nearly one year after Casserly was hired, the Texans finally named a coach. Dom Capers became the team's first head coach on January 21, 2001. Capers was selected because of his experience in building teams from scratch. He had been the head coach of the expansion Carolina Panthers from 1995 to 1998. He even guided the Panthers to the NFC Championship Game in their second year in the league.

A PLAN THAT FAILED

When the Texans selected Tony Boselli in the 2002 NFL Expansion Draft, they thought they would have a future Hall of Fame left tackle to protect their quarterback. Boselli had been the first-ever college draft choice in Jaguars history in 1995. The Jaguars were an expansion team that began playing in the NFL that year. Boselli went on to allow only 15.5 sacks in his first seven NFL seasons.

So, why had the Jaguars made him available to the Texans in the expansion draft? It was because Boselli played in only three games in 2001 due to injuries. He was coming off surgeries to both shoulders.

Boselli was never able to recover from the shoulder injuries. He missed the entire 2002 season and officially retired in 2003. He never took the field in a Texans uniform.

CARR GIVEN FRANCHISE'S KEYS

When David Carr was selected with the first pick in the 2002 NFL Draft, he made history in a couple of different ways. He was the first-ever college draft choice of the Texans. He was also the first Fresno State athlete to be a number one selection in any sport. Carr was coming off a standout senior season for the Bulldogs. He won the Johnny Unitas Award, the Football News Offensive Player of the Year award, and the Sammy Baugh Trophy. He also was the Western Athletic Conference Player of the Year after leading the nation in passing yards (4,308) and touchdowns (42). He became only the sixth NCAA Division I player ever to pass for 4,000 yards and 40 touchdowns in a season.

The Texans now had a nickname and logo. A state-of-the-art stadium was being built. Team colors had been chosen. A head coach had been hired. But there were still no players.

The team held workouts for free agents at the Astrodome. A few players were signed. Then the NFL held an expansion draft in February 2002. The Texans were allowed to choose from a group of players made available by other NFL teams. Five-time Pro Bowl player Tony Boselli, an offensive tackle with the Jacksonville Jaguars, was Houston's first pick.

"We have a Hall of Famer, and we haven't played a game," Casserly said.

The Texans selected 18 other players in the expansion draft. Offensive tackle Ryan Young, cornerbacks Aaron Glenn and Marcus Coleman, defensive tackles Gary Walker and Seth Payne, and linebacker Jamie Sharper all became important players for Houston. Unfortunately for the Texans, Boselli never played in a single game for them because of shoulder problems.

Two months later, with the first selection in the NFL

DAVID CARR HUGS HIS MOTHER, SHERYL, AFTER THE TEXANS SELECTED THE FORMER FRESNO STATE QUARTERBACK WITH THE FIRST OVERALL PICK IN THE 2002 NFL DRAFT.

Draft, the Texans chose David Carr. Carr had been a stand-out quarterback at Fresno State University. The Texans selected 11 other players in that 2002 college draft. But it was Carr who quickly became the face of the team. He signed a contract with the club on the day of the draft. Carr's play in the coming years would be an important factor in whether the Texans succeeded.

CHAPTER 3

UPS AND DOWNS

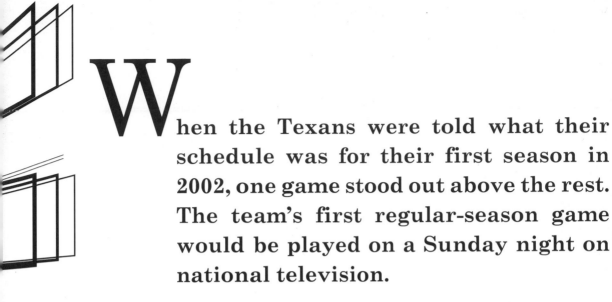

When the Texans were told what their schedule was for their first season in 2002, one game stood out above the rest. The team's first regular-season game would be played on a Sunday night on national television.

The opponent would be the Dallas Cowboys, a team for which many Houston football fans have no love.

"This game goes way beyond Cal-Stanford levels, and that's saying a lot," Texans linebacker Kailee Wong said. Wong went to Stanford University and played against the University of California in an annual rivalry known as "The Game." "But that's kind of what this game feels like here. It's kind of like in college, where you have that one big game, and it doesn't matter how you do for the rest of the season, as long as you win that game.

QUARTERBACK DAVID CARR IS PUMPED UP FOR THE TEXANS' FIRST REGULAR-SEASON GAME, A 19–10 WIN OVER THE COWBOYS ON SEPTEMBER 8, 2002.

WHO NEEDS AN OFFENSE?

On December 8, 2002, the visiting Texans defeated the Pittsburgh Steelers 24-6. Amazingly, the Texans won despite losing one fumble, giving up four sacks, gaining a team-worst 47 yards on offense, and allowing 422 yards on defense. How did Houston prevail? Cornerback Aaron Glenn returned two interceptions for touchdowns and the defense forced five turnovers.

"You get the sense from the fans that this is our big game. It's pretty important to them. It would be huge, absolutely huge, if we won. Our fans would go nuts."

The sellout crowd of 69,604 at Houston's new facility, Reliant Stadium, was going nuts before the game against the Cowboys even started on September 8, 2002. Fans showed up more than four hours early with their faces painted in Texans colors.

On the field, Houston quickly showed that it was ready to compete in the NFL.

On the first play from scrimmage in Texans history, Carr threw a deep pass to wide receiver Corey Bradford. The pass was incomplete. But pass interference was called. That moved Houston 43 yards to Dallas' 21-yard line.

Three plays later, Texans fans went delirious when tight end Billy Miller hauled in a 19-yard pass from Carr for the first touchdown in team history. The Texans then built a 10–0 lead in the second quarter on Kris Brown's 42–yard field goal.

Dallas came back and tied the score midway through the third quarter. But Houston scored on a 65-yard pass from Carr to Bradford on the opening drive of the fourth quarter. Nose tackle Seth Payne then sacked Cowboys quarterback Quincy Carter in the end zone for a safety with 2:37 remaining to give the

TEXANS CORNERBACK AARON GLENN ACKNOWLEDGES THE FANS AT RELIANT STADIUM IN HOUSTON'S 19–10 WIN OVER DALLAS TO OPEN THE 2002 SEASON.

Texans a 19–10 lead. They held on to win by that score.

The excitement did not last long. Houston lost its next five games before it defeated

DID YOU KNOW?

The Texans became only the second expansion team to win its first game. The Minnesota Vikings were the first team to accomplish the feat by beating the Chicago Bears in 1961.

HOUSTON'S ANDRE JOHNSON, *RIGHT*, BATTLES NEW ENGLAND'S TYRONE POOLE IN 2003. JOHNSON FINISHED HIS ROOKIE SEASON WITH 976 RECEIVING YARDS.

Jacksonville 21–19 on a late field goal by Brown. The win was the Texans' first in a road game. Houston won only two more games the rest of the season to finish 4–12. One victory came against the Pittsburgh Steelers. The Texans won 24–6 despite not scoring an offensive touchdown.

With the Texans' arrival in 2002, the NFL created four divisions in both the AFC and the NFC. Previously, each conference had three divisions. Joining Houston in the AFC South were the Indianapolis Colts, Jacksonville Jaguars, and Tennessee Titans. The Texans would play each of those teams twice a season. In its first season, Houston finished last in the division.

With the first season history, the Texans were looking forward to 2003. They believed that they would be an improved team. Carr would have a full season of experience. Domanick Davis, a running back, and Andre Johnson, a wide receiver, were drafted to give the offense more talent.

The Texans again won their season opener, defeating the Miami Dolphins 21–20 on the road. Through the first 12 games, Houston was 5–7. But the Texans then lost their final four games to finish 5–11. Their record was one game better than their 4–12 mark in the 2002 season.

While the Texans did not do as well as they hoped for on the field, Davis and Johnson had outstanding rookie seasons.

Johnson, the team's first-round draft choice out of the University of Miami in Florida, had 66 receptions for 976 yards and four touchdowns. Davis, a former Louisiana State University standout drafted in the fourth round, rushed for 1,031 yards and eight touchdowns. That season, Davis became the first player in league history to win NFL Rookie of the Week honors four straight times.

HISTORY AGAIN

The Texans tied the Vikings once again for expansion team honors by sending two players to the Pro Bowl in the team's first season. Cornerback Aaron Glenn and defensive end Gary Walker were selected to play for the AFC squad. Houston was the first first-year expansion team to have representatives at the Pro Bowl since the New Orleans Saints in 1967, when all teams had to have at least one player selected.

AN NFL STAR FOR A SHORT TIME

Domanick Davis entered the NFL in 2003. He legally changed his last name to Williams, his mother's maiden name, late in 2006.

Davis was a small running back out of Louisiana State University. He burst onto the NFL scene in 2003 by rushing for 1,031 yards and eight touchdowns. The performance was good enough for him to be named the NFL Rookie of Year. Davis was even better in 2004. He rushed for a club-record 1,188 yards and 13 touchdowns. He added 588 receiving yards on 68 receptions.

In 2005, Davis ran for 976 yards in 11 games. He suffered a knee injury that required surgery. It would end his career. He reported to training camp in 2006 and said he was healthy. But he soon experienced swelling in his knee and needed more surgery. Davis had to miss the entire season. In March 2007, the Texans released him.

In 2004, the Texans gave fans hope that the team was about to turn the corner. Houston went 7–9. Carr had his best NFL season. He threw for a career-high 3,531 yards and 16 touchdowns. Johnson had 79 receptions for 1,142 yards and six touchdowns. Davis rushed for 1,188 yards and 13 touchdowns.

But any hopes of a successful season in 2005 were dashed early in the year. The Texans lost their first six games before beating Cleveland 19–16.

Another six-game losing streak followed before Houston defeated Arizona 30–19. The Texans finished the season with two more losses, including a 20–17 defeat to San Francisco in the season finale.

Houston finished with a league-worst 2–14 record. Not

SECOND-YEAR TEXANS PLAYER DOMANICK DAVIS RUNS AGAINST THE CHIEFS IN 2004. DAVIS RUSHED FOR 1,188 YARDS THAT SEASON.

long after the final game, owner Bob McNair fired Dom Capers, the only head coach the Texans had known.

"I think that we've under-achieved this season," McNair said. "I think that everyone expected us to do more."

CHAPTER 4

START OF A
NEW DIRECTION

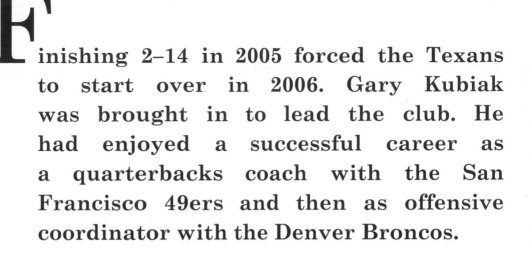

Finishing 2–14 in 2005 forced the Texans to start over in 2006. Gary Kubiak was brought in to lead the club. He had enjoyed a successful career as a quarterbacks coach with the San Francisco 49ers and then as offensive coordinator with the Denver Broncos.

One of the first decisions Kubiak and his staff had to make was deciding whom to take with the first selection in the 2006 NFL Draft. Heisman Trophy-winning running back Reggie Bush of the University of Southern California (USC) was available. So was quarterback Vince Young. Young had grown up in Houston and had guided the University of Texas to the national title. His Texas team beat Bush and USC in the national championship game. But, to the surprise of many, the Texans selected defensive end Mario Williams of North Carolina State University.

DEFENSIVE END MARIO WILLIAMS HOLDS UP A TEXANS JERSEY AFTER THE TEAM CHOSE HIM WITH THE NO. 1 OVERALL PICK IN THE 2006 NFL DRAFT.

NEEDING MORE OFFENSE

When the Texans hired Gary Kubiak to become the team's second head coach, one of the reasons was his background. Houston's offense struggled in 2005. Owner Bob McNair wanted a coach who could get the team to score more points.

Kubiak grew up in Houston, attending St. Pius High School. He then went on to star at Texas A&M University, where he played quarterback. In the NFL, he served as a backup to star John Elway with the Denver Broncos from 1983 to 1991. After a brief coaching stint at A&M, he joined George Seifert's staff with the San Francisco 49ers in 1994. Kubiak served as the quarterbacks coach and earned a Super Bowl ring. He then went to Denver when former San Francisco assistant Mike Shanahan was named the Broncos' coach. Kubiak became the team's offensive coordinator.

The move was not very popular with the fans in Houston. But Kubiak felt that he could help quarterback David Carr improve and that the team's biggest need was for a defensive player who could put pressure on opposing quarterbacks.

"This young man is special, what he brings to the game," Kubiak said of Williams. "He can change a game the way he rushes a passer and the problems he presents for an offensive football team."

With Williams now anchoring the defensive line, the defense as a whole played better in 2006. The offense showed some improvement as well. The Texans finished 6–10. They won four more games than they had the previous season.

Linebacker DeMeco Ryans had been drafted in the second

HOUSTON LINEBACKER DEMECO RYANS WRAPS UP DALLAS RUNNING BACK JULIUS JONES IN 2006. RYANS MADE AN IMMEDIATE IMPACT FOR THE TEXANS AS A ROOKIE.

round in 2006 to team with Williams. Ryans was a former University of Alabama standout. He made 125 tackles as a rookie with the Texans. On offense, Andre Johnson had his best year yet with 103 receptions for 1,147 yards and five touchdowns. Rookie tight end Owen Daniels added 34 catches for 352 yards and five touchdowns.

However, the expected improvement from Carr did not happen. He passed for only 2,767 yards and 11 touchdowns with 12 interceptions. After the season, the Texans released Carr after they acquired quarterback Matt Schaub in a trade with the Atlanta Falcons.

The Falcons had selected Schaub in the third round of

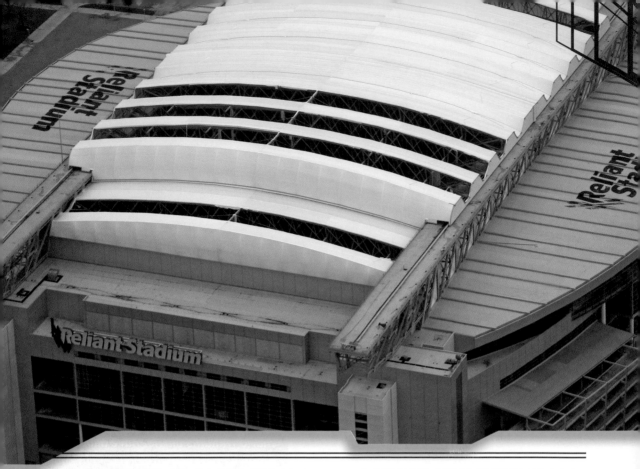

DAMAGE TO RELIANT STADIUM CAUSED BY HURRICANE IKE IS SHOWN IN THIS PHOTO FROM SEPTEMBER 13, 2008. THE TEXANS' SECOND GAME THAT SEASON, SCHEDULED FOR SEPTEMBER 14, WAS POSTPONED.

the 2004 NFL Draft. He had been a standout at the University of Virginia. Schaub was a backup with Atlanta from 2004 to 2006. He did not play much with the Falcons. But the Texans liked what they saw of him. They believed that he could be a good starting quarterback in the NFL if he were given the chance. To acquire Schaub, Houston gave its 2007 first-round pick (eighth overall) and second-round selections in 2007 and 2008 to Atlanta. The Falcons gave the Texans their 2007 first-round pick (10th overall).

The Texans showed their faith in Schaub when they gave him a six-year, $48 million contract. It was the beginning of a new era in Houston. The trio of Schaub, Johnson, and Daniels was expected to help carry the Texans to new heights. Daniels improved in 2007, making 63 catches for 768 yards. Johnson and Schaub, however, were limited because of injuries. Johnson played in only nine games. Schaub was limited to 11. Despite having two of their top offensive players out for part of the season, the Texans won a team-record eight games. Williams led the way on defense with 14 sacks. Houston avoided finishing with a losing record for the first time in team history.

The team had high hopes in 2008. But the season was dramatically altered in the early morning hours of September 13.

That is when Hurricane Ike made landfall near Galveston Bay and roared right through Houston. The hurricane damaged the roof at Reliant Stadium. The Texans had lost their season-opening game, 38–17 at Pittsburgh on September 7. Houston's second game of the season was scheduled to be for September 14 at home against the Baltimore Ravens. It had to be postponed

PROVING HIS VALUE

Mario Williams did not have a lot of fans when he first came to Houston in 2006. Texans followers wanted either Reggie Bush or Vince Young to be drafted with the first selection, not Williams. The 6-foot-6, 295-pound defensive end had a lot to prove. He struggled his first year with the team, as he managed only 4.5 sacks. But in 2007, he showed why the Texans wanted him to anchor the defensive line. He had 59 tackles in his second season and, more importantly, added 14 sacks. He followed that season with 53 tackles and 12 sacks in 2008. He came through with 43 tackles and nine sacks in 2009, despite being double-teamed on nearly every pass play.

ROOKIE OF THE YEAR

While Mario Williams was the big-name addition to the Texans' defense in 2006, a relatively unknown linebacker out of the University of Alabama stole the show that season and has been a defensive leader since. DeMeco Ryans, whom the Texans drafted with the first pick in the second round of the draft, was named the Associated Press Defensive Rookie of the Year in 2006. He received 72 percent of the votes and became the first Texans player to win the award. Through 2009, he had been named to the Pro Bowl twice (for the 2007 and 2009 seasons).

until November 9 because of the hurricane. As a result, the Texans would end up playing three road games to start the season.

In the two weeks after the hurricane, Houston lost to Tennessee and then to Jacksonville. The Texans finally came home to play at Reliant Stadium on October 5. But Indianapolis won 31–27. The Colts scored 21 unanswered points in the fourth quarter to pull out the victory and stun the Texans.

Houston was resilient. The team regrouped and defeated visiting Miami 29–28 the next week on Schaub's 3-yard touchdown run with three seconds left. Then came victories over the Detroit Lions and the Cincinnati Bengals. The Texans were suddenly 3–4. The up-and-down play of the team would be its theme in 2008. The three-game winning streak was followed by a three-game losing skid. But then the Texans won four straight games to improve to 7–7.

With two games remaining, Houston was in position to have a winning season for the first time. But the visiting Texans lost 27–16 to an Oakland Raiders team that was struggling. In the finale, host Houston beat the Chicago Bears 31–24. The Texans finished 8–8 for the second consecutive season.

QUARTERBACK MATT SCHAUB CELEBRATES HIS LATE 3-YARD TOUCHDOWN RUN THAT ALLOWED HOST HOUSTON TO BEAT MIAMI 29–28 IN OCTOBER 2008.

After two straight years of getting so close to having a winning season, fans were wondering whether the Texans were going to become a winning team. The next year would finally be the one in which Houston would finish better than .500. But the road to a winning season was not easy.

DID YOU KNOW?

On December 19, 2006, Andre Johnson was named as a starter for the AFC in the Pro Bowl. It was Johnson's second selection to the Pro Bowl in three seasons and the first time a Texans player had been named a starter in the game in team history.

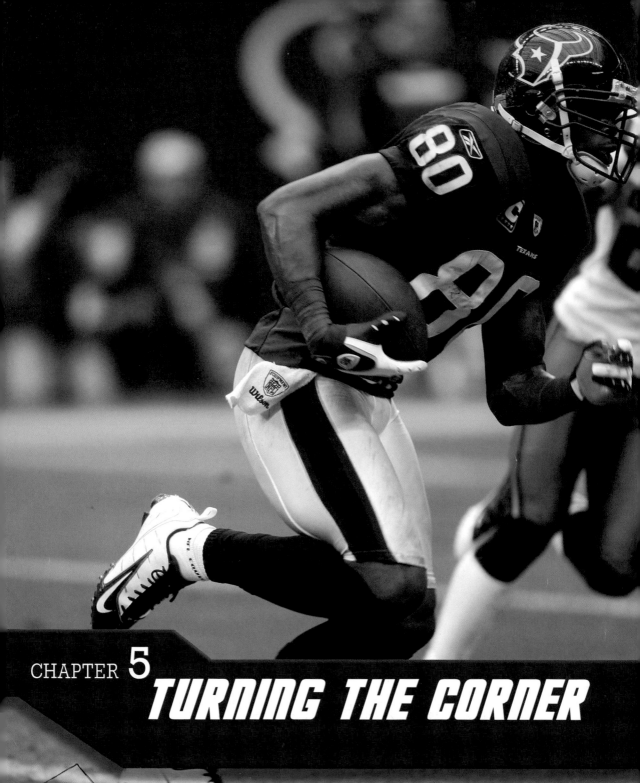

CHAPTER 5

TURNING THE CORNER

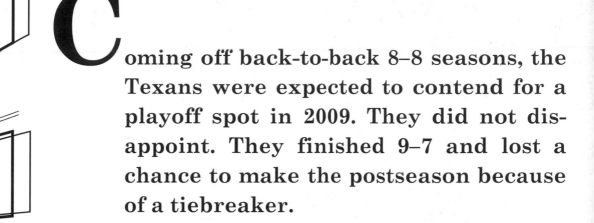

Coming off back-to-back 8–8 seasons, the Texans were expected to contend for a playoff spot in 2009. They did not disappoint. They finished 9–7 and lost a chance to make the postseason because of a tiebreaker.

But the fact that the Texans were able to finish with a winning record was somewhat amazing considering the bad luck and injuries the team experienced. After a loss to the New York Jets to start the season, Houston came back to win 34–31 at Tennessee in Week 2. However, during the game, left guard Chester Pitts suffered what turned out to be a season-ending right knee injury. Pitts was an original Texans player. He was drafted by the club in 2002. Including the game against the Titans, he had started in every game in team history—a string of 114 games.

"It was a big adjustment all year long, because when you

ANDRE JOHNSON RUNS WITH THE BALL DURING THE TEXANS' 34–7 WIN OVER THE SEAHAWKS IN DECEMBER 2009. JOHNSON HAD 101 CATCHES THAT SEASON.

LOSING AN ANCHOR

When Chester Pitts was lost for the season after suffering an injury to his right knee during the second week of the 2009 season, the Texans lost their starting left guard. They also lost one of the most reliable players in club history.

Drafted by the Texans in 2002, Pitts had started every game in team history, a streak of 114 games. Pitts needed two surgeries to repair the knee.

"Those are some big shoes to fill," said Kasey Studdard, the man who replaced Pitts. "He's our iron man." Kris Brown, the team's kicker, was the only other player on the roster who had been with the team since its first season in 2002. "My heart goes out to Chester," Brown said. "He's meant so much to this organization. He's put so much into this team through the years that it just breaks your heart to see this happen."

lose Chester, what you're losing is a big, physical player that handles three techniques and is very stout on the line of scrimmage," coach Gary Kubiak said. "He was a leader, also. So we started adjusting."

Houston suffered another setback when right guard Mike Brisiel sustained a season-ending injury. With two starters out on the offensive line, the Texans' running game was not very effective. Houston sputtered to a 2–3 start. However, mainly behind the success of their passing game, the Texans went on a three-game winning streak. They improved to 5–3. They were two games over .500 for the first time in team history.

But in the third win of that streak, a 31–10 rout of the host Buffalo Bills, tight end Owen Daniels suffered a season-end-

TEXANS MEDICAL STAFF MEMBERS EXAMINE TIGHT END OWEN DANIELS'S RIGHT KNEE ON NOVEMBER 1, 2009. DANIELS HURT THE KNEE AGAINST THE BILLS AND WOULD MISS THE REST OF THE SEASON.

ing injury. He tore a ligament in his right knee. Daniels was coming off a Pro Bowl season in 2008 in which he had made 70 catches for 862 yards. Daniels was playing just as well in 2009. He had 40 receptions for 519 yards and five touchdowns eight games

into the season. "It's a big blow to our football team," Kubiak said. "I just feel bad for him. He was having a tremendous season, a special football season, and we're going to miss him big time."

Houston's offense became less successful. After averaging

LINEBACKER BRIAN CUSHING MADE 133 TACKLES IN 2009 AND WAS
NAMED THE NFL DEFENSIVE ROOKIE OF THE YEAR.

BREAKOUT PERFORMANCE

Quarterback Matt Schaub started all 16 games in 2009, even though he suffered a separated left shoulder during the season. Schaub earned a spot in the Pro Bowl after throwing for a league-leading 4,770 yards and 29 touchdowns.

24.8 points through the first eight games of the season, the Texans averaged only 19.8 in their next four games. All four of those games were losses. Houston dropped to 5–7. The team's chances of having a winning season were looking doubtful. The only way that the Texans would finish above .500 would be to win the final four games of the season.

The Texans embarked on a very strong finish. This was the result of the strong passing of Matt Schaub, the receiving skills of Andre Johnson, and the defensive tenacity of Mario Williams, DeMeco Ryans, and standout rookie linebacker Brian Cushing. Houston took apart the visiting Seattle Seahawks 34–7 to improve to 6–7. The Texans then defeated the St. Louis Rams 16–13 on the road to even their record at 7–7. Houston then had another road test, in Miami. The Texans defeated the Dolphins 27–20. Houston had moved one game over .500 with one game left to play.

The Texans went on to defeat the New England Patriots in the

ROOKIE SENSATION

The Texans selected former University of Southern California standout linebacker Brian Cushing in the first round of the 2009 NFL Draft. They expected him to be a fast and physical player who could be a force on defense. Cushing did not disappoint. A starter from the day he entered camp, Cushing had 133 tackles and was named the NFL Defensive Rookie of the Year. He joined fellow Houston linebacker DeMeco Ryans as Texans to capture that award. Ryans won it in 2006.

season's last game to finish with their first winning record. The club fell short of the postseason, however. This left Houston with an even higher goal: make the playoffs. Now a winning team, becoming a playoff squad was the next mountain the Texans would try to conquer. With highly talented players such as Schaub, Johnson, and Williams leading the way, the team's future appeared very promising.

TIMELINE

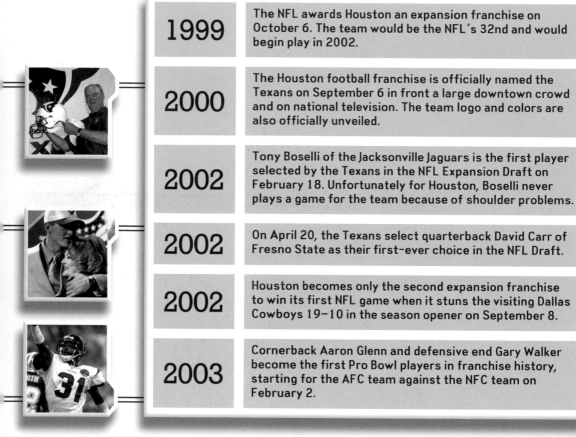

1999	The NFL awards Houston an expansion franchise on October 6. The team would be the NFL's 32nd and would begin play in 2002.
2000	The Houston football franchise is officially named the Texans on September 6 in front a large downtown crowd and on national television. The team logo and colors are also officially unveiled.
2002	Tony Boselli of the Jacksonville Jaguars is the first player selected by the Texans in the NFL Expansion Draft on February 18. Unfortunately for Houston, Boselli never plays a game for the team because of shoulder problems.
2002	On April 20, the Texans select quarterback David Carr of Fresno State as their first-ever choice in the NFL Draft.
2002	Houston becomes only the second expansion franchise to win its first NFL game when it stuns the visiting Dallas Cowboys 19–10 in the season opener on September 8.
2003	Cornerback Aaron Glenn and defensive end Gary Walker become the first Pro Bowl players in franchise history, starting for the AFC team against the NFC team on February 2.

2003   Running back Domanick Davis is named the NFL Rookie of the Year for the 2003 season.

2005   Wide receiver Andre Johnson, on February 13, becomes the first Texans offensive player to play in the Pro Bowl.

2006   Linebacker DeMeco Ryans becomes the first Texans player to earn NFL Defensive Rookie of the Year honors.

2007   The Associated Press names Ryans and defensive end Mario Williams to its All-Pro second team for the 2007 season. They are the first Texans position players named to the team. Kick returner Jerome Mathis was selected as a first-team All-Pro in 2005.

2008   Johnson is named to the Associated Press All-Pro first team. He becomes the first Texans position player to earn the honor. Johnson led the NFL with 115 receptions for 1,575 yards in 2008.

2009   Linebacker Brian Cushing is named the NFL Defensive Rookie of the Year for the 2009 season. He becomes the second Texans linebacker to win the award.

QUICK STATS

FRANCHISE HISTORY

2002–

SUPER BOWLS

None

DIVISION CHAMPIONSHIPS

None

PLAYOFF APPEARANCES

None

KEY PLAYERS
(position, seasons with team)

Kris Brown (K, 2002–)
David Carr (QB, 2002–06)
Owen Daniels (TE, 2006–)
Domanick Davis (Williams)
   (RB, 2003–05)
Aaron Glenn (CB, 2002–04)
Andre Johnson (WR, 2003–)
Chester Pitts (OL, 2002–)
Dunta Robinson (CB, 2004–09)
DeMeco Ryans (LB, 2006–)
Matt Schaub (QB, 2007–)
Mario Williams (DE, 2006–)

KEY COACHES

Dom Capers (2002–05): 18–46–0
Gary Kubiak (2006–): 31–33–0

HOME FIELDS

Reliant Stadium (2002–)

* All statistics through 2009 season

"Now they can go back to Dallas and have a hard-knock life. We ruined their season."
—Defensive end Gary Walker, after Houston defeated the Dallas Cowboys in the Texans' first-ever regular-season game in 2002

"I am retiring because of medical reasons, specifically my left shoulder, which did not continue to improve to the point where I could play. I am disappointed that I will not be able to play for the Texans and do what I was brought here to do."
—Offensive tackle Tony Boselli, Houston's first choice in the 2002 NFL Expansion Draft, announcing his retirement in 2003

"This is another exciting moment in the history of the Texans. Winning is all about getting better every day, and that's what we're trying to do."
—Houston owner Bob McNair, after the club traded for and then signed quarterback Matt Schaub to a long-term contract in 2007

"That's the toughest thing I'm dealing with now, knowing that we had opportunities. A game here, a game there, a play here, a play there. You kind of knew those would come back and haunt us, and that's what happened. . . . It's a real painful lesson to have to learn. But you learn it and move on."
—Linebacker DeMeco Ryans, talking about the missed chances the Texans had during the 2009 season, forcing them to rely on other teams to help them get into the playoffs. That did not happen.

GLOSSARY

All-Pro

An award given to the top players at their positions, regardless of their conference. It is a high honor as there are fewer spots on the All-Pro team than on the Pro Bowl teams.

American Football Conference

One of two conferences that make up the NFL. As of 2010, there were 16 teams in the AFC.

berth

A place, spot, or position, such as in the NFL playoffs.

contend

To compete.

contract

A binding agreement about, for example, years of commitment by a football player in exchange for a given salary.

expansion

In sports, to add a franchise or franchises to a league.

franchise

An entire sports organization, including the players, coaches, and staff.

Heisman Trophy

An award given to the top college football player each year.

National Football Conference

One of the conferences that make up the NFL. As of 2010, there were 16 teams in the NFC.

Pro Bowl

A game after the regular season in which the top players from the AFC play against the top players from the NFC.

rookie

A first-year professional athlete.

sack

Term used when a defensive player tackles the quarterback behind the line of scrimmage.

FOR MORE INFORMATION

Further Reading

MacCambridge, Michael. *America's Game: The Epic Story of How Pro Football Captured a Nation*. New York: Random House, 2004.

Sports Illustrated. *The Football Book Expanded Edition*. New York: Sports Illustrated Books, 2009.

Toole, Carter. *Opening Night*. New York: Houston NFL Holdings, 2002.

Web Links

To learn more about the Houston Texans, visit ABDO Publishing Company online at **www.abdopublishing.com**. Web sites about the Texans are featured on our Book Links page. These links are routinely monitored and updated to provide the most current information available.

Places to Visit

Pro Football Hall of Fame
2121 George Halas Drive NW
Canton, OH 44708
330-456-8207
www.profootballhof.com
This hall of fame and museum highlights the greatest players and moments in the history of the National Football League. As of 2010, no one affiliated with the Texans was enshrined.

Reliant Stadium
One Reliant Park
Houston, TX 77054
832-667-1842
www.reliantpark.com/reliantstadium
This is where the Texans play all their home games.

Texans Training Camp
Methodist Training Center at Reliant Park
One Reliant Park
Houston, TX 77054
832-667-2323
This facility, next to Reliant Stadium, is where the Texans hold their training camp in the summer and also where they practice during the season.

INDEX

About the Author

J Chris Roselius has been an award-winning writer and journalist for more than 15 years. A graduate of the University of Texas, he has written numerous books. Currently residing in Houston, Texas, he enjoys spending time with his wife and two children.